The QUILTED CROSS

J. Michelle Watts

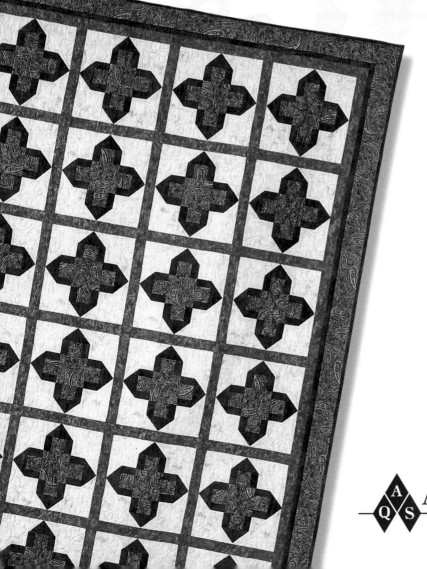

American Quilter's Society

P. O. Box 3290 • Paducah, KY 42002-3290

www.AQSquilt.com

Located in Paducah, Kentucky, the American Quilter's Society (AQS) is dedicated to promoting the accomplishments of today's quilters. Through its publications and events, AQS strives to honor today's quiltmakers and their work and to inspire future creativity and innovation in quiltmaking.

EDITOR: BARBARA SMITH
GRAPHIC DESIGN: AMY CHASE
COVER DESIGN: MICHAEL BUCKINGHAM
PHOTOGRAPHY: CHARLES R. LYNCH

Library of Congress Cataloging-in-Publication Data

Watts, J. Michells, 1959-
    The quilted cross / by J. Michelle Watts.
        p. cm.
      ISBN 1-57432-832-8
  1. Patchwork--Patterns. 2. Quilting. 3. Appliqué--Patterns. 4.
Redwork. 5. Crosses in art. I. Title.

TT835.W37597 2003
746.46'041--dc22

                    2003019899

Additional copies of this book may be ordered from the American Quilter's Society, PO Box 3290, Paducah, KY 42002-3290, or online at www.AQSquilt.com.

Dedication

This book is dedicated to my husband, Randy, and to my daughter, Jessica. I thank each of them for their support, patience, and encouragement. My life would be empty without them.

Acknowledgments

I would like to thank all my friends for all their help. You helped me proof-read instructions, made blocks, gave me advice, and helped by making some of the sample quilts.

I want to express a very special thank you to my dear friend, Marion. You are always there for me.

Thank you to all my students for their continuing support and interest in all the classes I teach and patterns I design.

To my friend, Mary Jo, thank you for your friendship and guidance.

SPINNING CROSS (48" x 58"), pieced by Marion Wessel, Roswell, New Mexico. Machine quilted by Phyllis Kent, Los Lunas, New Mexico. Pattern begins on page 14.

Contents

Introduction

Some people collect cats, hearts, stars, bears, salt and pepper shakers, and other unique objects. We even know that there's a large group of people who collect fabric. Well, I like collecting crosses. For some unexplainable reason, I am drawn to them. My fascination with crosses began several years ago. I was browsing at a flea market and stopped at a jewelry vendor's booth. There before me was the most beautiful turquoise pendant I had ever seen. It was an incredible chunk of turquoise, carved into the shape of a simple cross, backed with ornate silver, and accented with amber. I bought it. And that was the beginning of my collection. Now,

ALEXIS SWOBODA (53" x 53"), by Alexis Swoboda, Roswell, New Mexico. Alexis pieced the Greek Cross block in several color combinations and set them together for a scrappy look.

my cross collection includes jewelry, sculptures, wall decorations, Christmas decorations, and best of all, quilts.

A Shining Light (20" x 20"), by the author. This cross represents the rays of hope that shine through in the darkest of times. Pieced chevrons frame the blocks in this wall quilt.

After I began creating embossed metal, wood, wire, and bead cross art for a small gallery, I quickly learned I wasn't the only person interested in collecting crosses. Then one day, I decided it was time to combine my love for quilting and my fascination with crosses. The first 12 designs I sketched became a beautiful quilt I named Las Cruces, which is Spanish for "the crosses." More designs followed, so you see that I'm just adding to my collection, and now maybe this can be the beginning of your cross collection.

The quilted cross designs I have presented here were inspired by a variety of sculptures, art, tinwork, ironwork, wood and stone carvings, beadwork, mission altars, churches, silverwork, pottery, jewelry, tiles, clay, architecture, cemetery art, religious symbols, medieval heraldry, and rock art. The patterns offered make up a collection of unique patchwork, appliqué, embroidery, and quilted cross patterns. The designs encompass a variety of traditional and contemporary blocks, which can be used to create elegant pillows, wallhangings, table runners, tablecloths, place mats, quilts, and wearable art.

Various techniques were used to make the blocks. The popularity of traditional redwork embroidery inspired me to create a few blocks for those who love to embroider. These will make a lovely pillow or wallhanging. In addition, I have included several easy-to-piece, traditional blocks for the traditionalists. There is a contemporary paper-pieced block for those with an interest in abstract design, and the Santa Cruz sampler blocks, on page 35, can be combined in any number or arrangement for a stunning creation. I have added interesting facts about crosses.

You have the freedom to choose the blocks you want to make and to select the color combination, block setting, borders, and quilting patterns for your quilts. The colors and fabrics you choose for each piece will determine the image or style of your quilt.

Crosses can be a symbol of religious or spiritual belief, or they can be viewed as purely ornamental. Every cross I see has its own sense of beauty, no matter how simple or complex, and I hope you will see the beauty in them and be inspired to explore the possibilities.

CROSS IN THE WINDOW (36" x 48"), by Pam Abbott, Columbus, Ohio. Pam used jewel-tone fabrics and added an exciting textural element with machine quilting.

JEWELED CROSS TRIO (15" x 45"), by the author. The black background dramatically changes the look of these Santa Cruz blocks.

Construction Tips

The pattern directions were written assuming that you know basic quiltmaking skills; however, the following tips may prove useful to you.

Fabrics

Cotton. I recommend 100 percent cotton fabrics. They are easy to handle and come in a wide variety of colors, patterns, and textures. For a little extra sparkle, try some cotton lamé, silk, or satin. Handle these fabrics carefully to keep them from stretching. A lightweight fusible interfacing can add stability to them.

Colors. The colors I have chosen for my projects express my love of the Southwest. Feel free to substitute your favorite colors.

Tools and Supplies

In addition to the basic sewing supplies — scissors, straight pins, and safety pins; good quality thread for sewing, appliqué, and quilting; and a good iron — you will need the following tools:

Rotary equipment. The pieced patterns provide measurements for rotary cutting. You will need a rotary cutter, mat, and clear acrylic ruler. My favorite is the 6" x 24" with 1/8" markings and 45° and 60° angle markings.

Fusible webbing. The appliqué projects can be machine appliquéd with fusible webbing and a narrow zigzag stitch. The zigzag stitches should be close together and even. For best results, consult your sewing machine manual.

Thread. The right thread is an important part of every project. I like to machine piece with 100 percent cotton thread. For machine appliqué, I use a silk-finish cotton or rayon thread with a lightweight bobbin thread.

Sewing machine. Your sewing machine needs to be in good working order. It is important that the machine makes evenly locked straight stitches for piecing. I set my stitch length to about 12 stitches per inch.

Making Blocks

Pieced blocks. Use 1/4" seam allowances, unless otherwise stated.

Half-square triangle units. To piece half-square triangle units, layer two squares (sizes given in the patterns), right sides together, with the lightest square on top. Draw a diagonal line on the wrong side of the top square. Sew a 1/4" seam allowance on both sides of the drawn line. Cut on the drawn line to form two identical pieced squares (fig. 1).

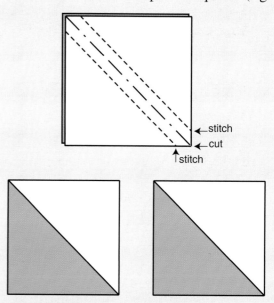

Fig. 1. Half-square triangle units

Flying Geese units. My Flying Geese unit is pieced with a rectangle and two squares. Draw a diagonal line on the wrong side of each square. Place a square on one end of the rectangle, with right sides together. Sew on the diagonal line. Trim away the excess fabric, leaving a ¼" seam allowance. Press the seam allowances toward the triangle. Repeat for the other end of the rectangle (fig. 2)

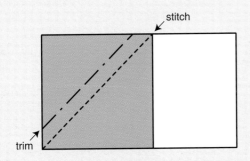

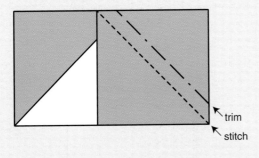

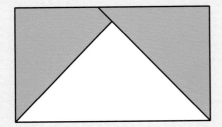

Fig. 2. Flying Geese unit

Appliqué. The appliqué patterns can be used at the size given or enlarged as desired. The percentage of enlargement provided is for making blocks the same size as those in the quilt photos.

Master pattern. You will need a master pattern for the appliqué designs. Enlarge the appliqué patterns as instructed for the block size given or as needed for your project. Keep the enlargement as your master pattern and make a second copy to cut apart for templates. If you prefer, pattern pieces can also be traced directly onto the paper side of fusible webbing.

Foundation piecing. The lines in the paper-foundation piecing pattern are sewing lines.

Hand embroidery. I recommend using two strands of hand embroidery thread and the traditional outline stitch.

Machine embroidery. I use the triple stitch or jeans stitch with a good quality cotton thread on the top and in the bobbin. You can also try using the simple straight stitch with two matching threads in the same needle. I recommend shortening your stitch length for more control around curves and corners.

Sashing and borders. Don't be afraid to experiment with setting your blocks together in different arrangements and adding sashings and borders to make your project any size you desire. The type of sashings and borders added can dramatically affect the finished look of the quilt.

Quilting. You can quilt the layers by machine or by hand.

Pieced Crosses
Greek Cross
Finished block 9"

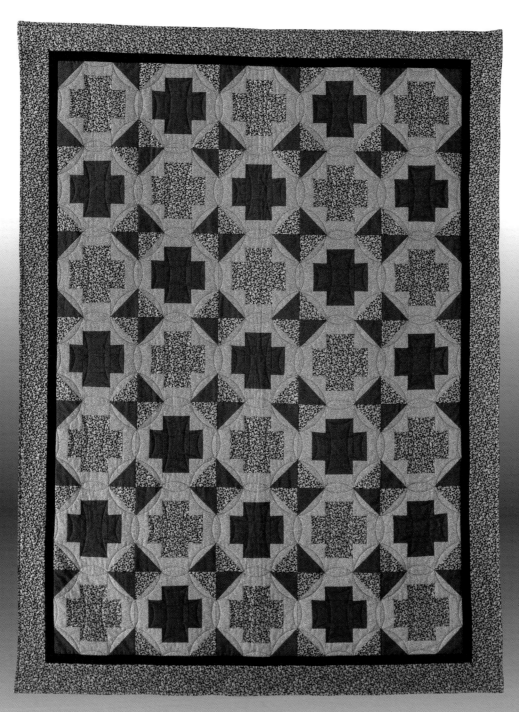

GREEK CROSS (53" x 71"), pieced by the author and machine quilted by Phyllis Kent, Los Lunas, New Mexico. In the Greek cross form, the horizontal and vertical shafts are equal in size. In this wall quilt, alternating colors create secondary patterns.

The Greek cross is one of the original forms used by Christians. Before Christianity, this cross was an emblem of the Greek goddess of crossroads, Hecate. The Greek Cross block is an old traditional pattern, and it is an excellent block for a beginner. I recommend piecing this block with three high-contrast fabrics. For a scrappier version, try piecing a variety of different colored crosses with the same background fabric.

Cutting Instructions (one block)

Fabric	Cut	From one scrap
White print	2 squares	3⅞" x 3⅞"
	1 strip	2" x 18"
Red & black print	2 squares	3⅞" x 3⅞"
Red	1 square	3½" x 3½"
	1 strip	2" x 18"

1. Piece four identical, 3½" half-square triangle units from the 3⅞" squares (fig. 3).

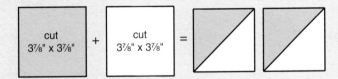

Fig. 3. Make 4 units.

2. Sew the strips into a strip-set as shown (fig. 4). Press the seam allowances toward the darkest fabric. Cut the strip-set into four 3½" squares.

3. Referring to the block assembly diagram (fig. 5), join the units in rows, then join the rows together to complete the block.

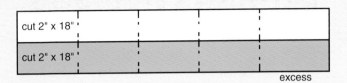

Fig. 4. Cut the strip-set into 3½" squares.

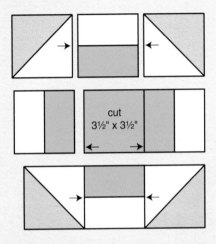

Fig. 5. Block assembly. Arrows indicate seam allowance pressing.

Spinning Cross

Finished block 10"

SPINNING CROSS (58" x 71), by the author. My inspiration for this block was the Zia symbol in the New Mexico state flag. I just made it look like it was spinning.

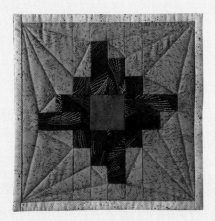

A cross is a universal symbol for the sun. The four arms can represent the four directions: north, east, south and west. I recommend piecing this block in three different fabrics. For a scrappy quilt, piece different strip-sets and mix them up for each block.

Cutting Instructions (one block)

Fabric	Cut	From one scrap
Turquoise	1 rectangle	3½" x 8"
	1 rectangle	1½" x 8"
	1 rectangle	2½" x 8"
	4 rectangles	3½" x 4½"
Black print	1 rectangle	1½" x 8"
	1 rectangle	3½" x 8"
	1 rectangle	2½" x 8"
Red	1 square	2½" x 2½"

1. Piece strip-sets A, B, and C from the turquoise and the black rectangles. Cut each strip-set into four sections 1½" wide (fig. 6).

2. Referring to the block assembly diagram (fig. 7), piece the units. Sew the units into rows, then join the rows to complete the block.

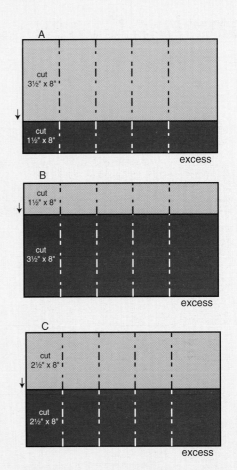

Fig. 6. Strip-sets. Cut into 1½" sections. Arrows indicate seam allowance pressing.

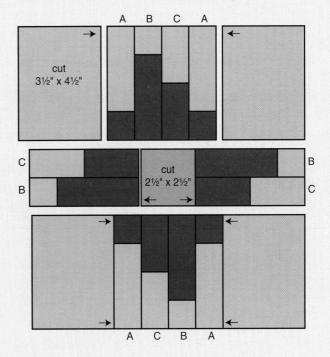

Fig. 7. Block assembly

St. Anne's Cross

Finished block 12"

ST. ANNE'S CROSS (80" x 94"), pieced by the author and machine quilted by Phyllis Kent, Los Lunas, New Mexico. I chose rich, elegant purples and royal blues for this quilt block, which provided the perfect place to showcase a paisley print.

The cross can be symbolic of the merging of opposites and the connection between heaven and earth. The cross can also be a symbol of many different things. The tree of life, crucifixion, suffering, redemption, and faith are just a few.

Cutting Instructions (one block)

Fabric	Cut	From one scrap
Light pink	8 squares	2½" x 2½"
	4 squares	4½" x 4½"
Dark purple	2 strips	1½" x 13"
	4 rectangles	2½" x 4½"
Paisley print	1 strip	2½" x 13"
	1 square	4½" x 4½"

1. Piece one strip-set from the 13" long dark purple and paisley print strips (fig. 8). Press the seam allowances toward the darker fabric. Cut the strip-set into 4 sections 2½" wide.

3. Referring to the block assembly diagram (fig. 9), sew the Flying Geese, strip-set sections, and squares into rows. Sew the rows together to complete the block (fig. 9).

Fig. 9. Block assembly. Arrows indicate seam allowance pressing.

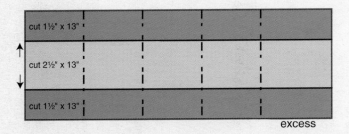

Fig. 8. Cut the strip-set into 2½" sections.

2. Use the dark purple rectangles and light pink squares to piece 4 identical Flying Geese units. (See Flying Geese units on page 11.)

Enchanted Cross

Finished block 13"

ENCHANTED CROSS (60" x 75"), by the author. This block was inspired by a heraldic cross.

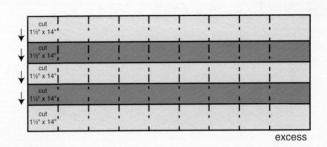

Fig. 10. Cut the strip-set into 1½" sections.

I recommend piecing this block in two highly contrasting fabrics. For a wall quilt, piece several blocks with a dark background and several with a light background, then alternate the blocks in each row. This block was enlarged by adding 1½" cut strips around it.

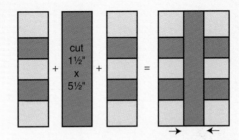

Fig. 11. Cross unit. Arrows indicate seam allowance pressing.

Cutting Instructions (one block)

Fabric	Cut	From one scrap
Beige	4 squares	5½" x 5½"
	3 strips	1½" x 14"
	1 square	1½" x 1½"
Red	2 strips	1½" x 14"
	4 rectangles	1½" x 5½"
	2 rectangles	1½" x 3½"
	2 squares	1½" x 1½"

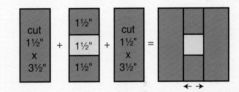

Fig. 12. Center square

1. Piece one strip-set from the 1½" x 14" strips (fig. 10). Press all the seam allowances in one direction. Cut the strip-set into 8 sections, 1½" wide.

2. Piece 4 identical cross units. Press the seam allowances toward the center (fig. 11).

3. Piece 1 center square unit (fig. 12).

4. Referring to the block assembly diagram, assemble the units into rows. Then sew the rows together to complete the block (fig. 13).

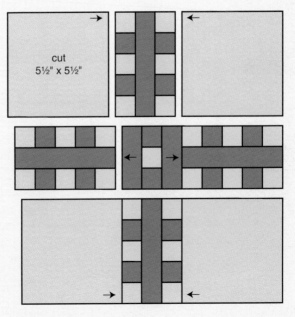

Fig. 13. Block assembly

Cross Crosslet

Finished block 9"

CROSS CROSSLET (50" x 60"), pieced by the author and machine quilted by Phyllis Kent, Los Lunas, New Mexico. The cross crosslet is a heraldic symbol. In this quilt, strips were added around the block to increase its size.

As a decorative unit, the cross has a long pre-Christian history and is found in both Eastern and Western cultures. Decorative crosses can be seen in Greek art and Roman floor mosaics.

Cutting Instructions (one block)

Fabric	Cut	From one scrap
Cream	4 squares	3½" x 3½"
	2 strips	1½" x 18"
Turquoise	1 strip	1½" x 18"
	5 rectangles	1½" x 3½"

1. Piece together one strip-set from the 1½" x18" rectangles. Press seam allowances in the same direction. Cut the strip-set into 10 sections, 1½" wide (fig. 14).

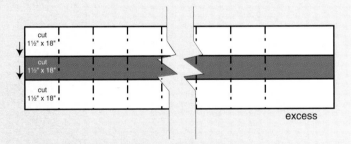

Fig. 14. Cut the strip-set into 1½" sections.

2. Piece five identical cross units (fig. 15). Press the seam allowances toward the center.

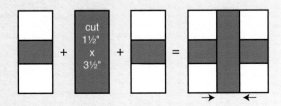

Fig. 15. Make 5 cross units. Arrows indicate seam allowance pressing.

3. Referring to the block assembly diagram, sew the units and squares into rows. Sew the rows together to complete the block (fig. 16).

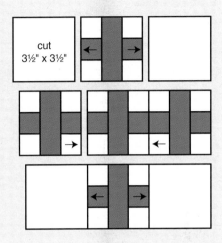

Fig. 16. Block assembly

Pressures of the World

Finished block 8"

(patterns on pages 23-25)

PRESSURES OF THE WORLD (31" x 39"), by the author. While in Germany, my daughter e-mailed me a photo of a crushed cross sculpture from the Evangelische Versöhnungskirche (Church of Reconciliation) in Dachau. I wanted to create a block that symbolized what my daughter saw. This design was the result.

This block is easy to piece by using the paper foundation technique. I prefer to precut all my fabric pieces before I start to sew, so I have given the cutting measurements needed for each piece. For a wall quilt with several blocks, use a variety of prints for the crosses.

Cutting Instructions (one block)

Fabric	Cut	From one scrap
Black	A2	2" x 3"
	A3	4½" x 4½"
	A4	4½" x 4½"
	B2	2" x 2"
	C2	1½" x 1½"
	C3	4½" x 4½"
	C4	5" x 5"
Contrasting print	A1	3" x 4"
	B1	3" x 8½"
	C1	3" x 4"

1. Trace the pattern lines on tracing paper or use an accurate photocopier to make as many copies as needed.

2. Piece the sections in numerical order. Trim the edges of each section, leaving a ¼" seam allowance on all sides.

3. Sew together sections A and B. Sew this unit to section C to form the quilt block.

4. Remove the paper from the block after it has been sewn to other blocks or the sashing has been added.

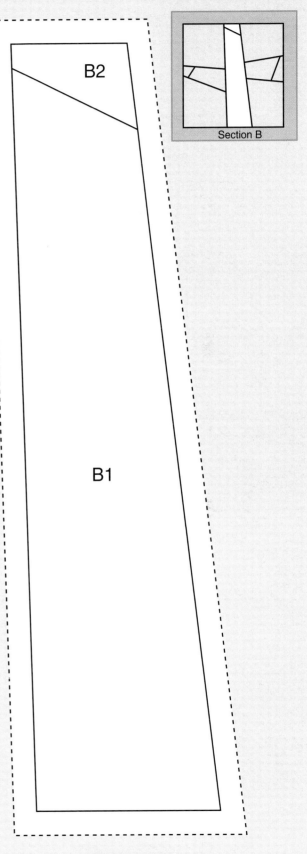

Section B

Section B

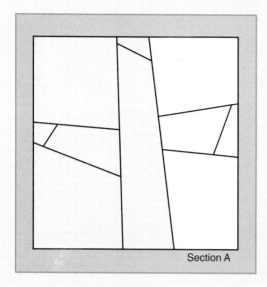

Section A

Pressures of the World

Full-sized paper foundation pattern. (Permission to copy as needed for non-commercial use.)

Place the cut fabric pieces (right side up) on the unmarked side of the pattern. Sew on the lines on the marked side.

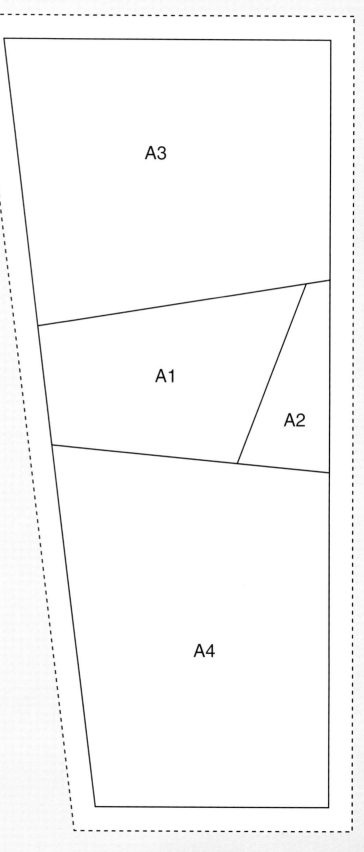

A3

A1

A2

A4

Section A

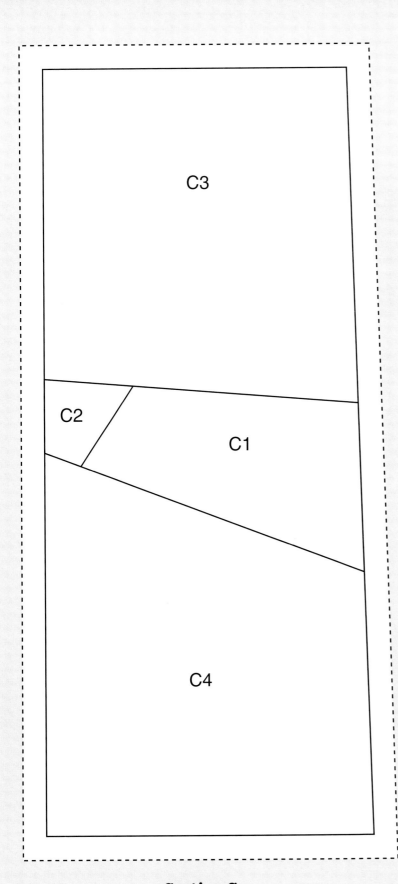

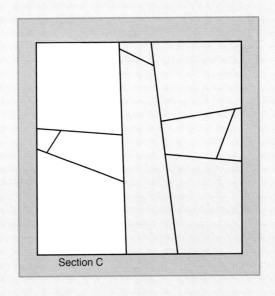

Section C

Section C

Appliquéd Crosses
Celtic Cross

Finished block 15½"

6 appliqué pieces (pattern on page 28)

CELTIC CROSS (38" x 38"), by the author. I drew the outside cross shape, then filled in the open space. I selected a large, bold print, which gave this quilt an Oriental flair.

The large pieces in this block make it a great project for a beginner. Choose a light background fabric. The outside cross shape should be cut from a strong, dark fabric for best results. Select a large, bold print for the interior or try a medium to large floral print for a softer look.

Cutting Instructions (one block)

Fabric	Cut	From one scrap
Background	1 square	17" x 17"
Black	1 A	17" x 17"
Red print	4 B	5" x 20"
	1 C	5" x 5"

The following steps are for raw-edge fusible appliqué. Use a photocopier to enlarge the pattern 200% for a 15 ½" block, or to any size you desire.

1. Use freezer paper or tracing paper to make a master pattern of the block on page 28.

2. Fold the background square into quarters and press. Use the pressed lines as guides for centering your appliqué pieces.

3. Trace each individual pattern piece onto the paper side of your favorite fusible web. (For pieces that will be covered by another piece, add a ¼" allowance to only the portion that will be covered.) Rough-cut each of the fusible web pieces.

4. Following the manufacturer's directions, iron the fusible web pattern pieces to the wrong sides of the appropriate fabrics.

5. Cut out all the fabric pieces on the drawn lines and carefully peel off the paper backing.

6. Position each appliqué piece on the background square. Fuse the pieces to the background according to the manufacturer's instructions.

7. Place a piece of freezer paper behind your background square to stabilize it for sewing.

8. Machine sew (in alphabetical order) the raw edges of each piece with a narrow zigzag stitch in matching thread. Tear away the stabilizer when your appliqué is complete.

9. Press the appliquéd block, then trim it to 16", which includes seam allowances.

AUTUMN WINDS (57" x 76"), appliquéd by Jamie Boling, Roswell, New Mexico, and machine quilted by Phyllis Kent, Los Lunas, New Mexico

Celtic Cross

To make a 15½" block, enlarge this pattern 200%.
(Permission to copy as needed for non-commercial use.)

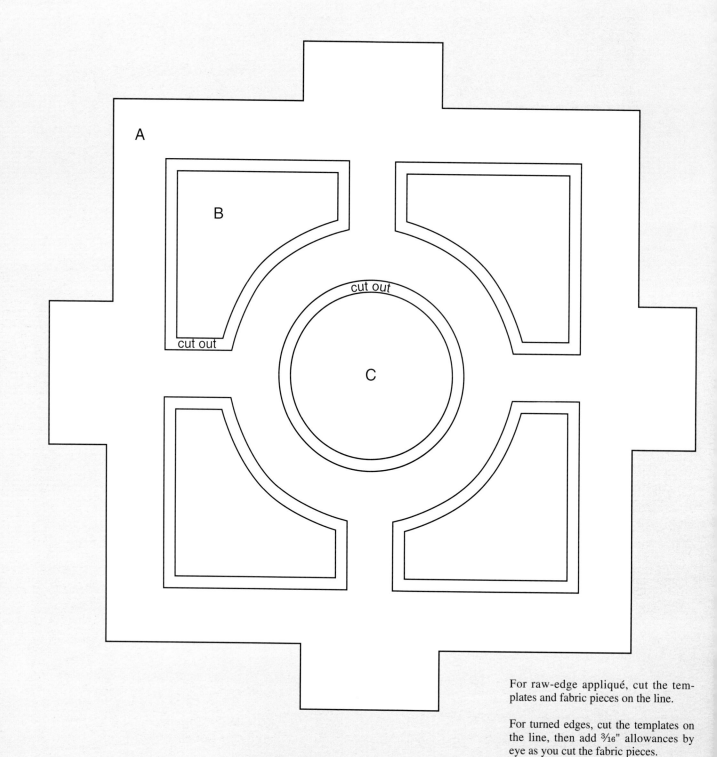

A

B

cut out

cut out

C

For raw-edge appliqué, cut the templates and fabric pieces on the line.

For turned edges, cut the templates on the line, then add ³⁄₁₆" allowances by eye as you cut the fabric pieces.

Shining Light

Finished block 16" x 20",
25 appliqué pieces
(pattern on page 31)

A SHINING LIGHT (40" x 44"), by Jan Hightower, Roswell, New Mexico. Jan selected earthy
Southwestern fabrics for her blocks.

Appliquéd Crosses

In the Latin cross form, the vertical shaft is longer than the cross shaft, and the cross shaft is usually two-thirds of the way up the vertical shaft. For a stained-glass effect, select a light background fabric and jewel-toned fabrics for the cross, then use a black satin stitch for the machine appliqué.

Cutting Instructions (one block)

Fabric	Cut	From one scrap
Cream	1 rectangle	18" x 22"
Black	4 A	3" x 6"
Brown	2 B & 2 Br	6" x 7"
	2 E & 2 Er	5" x 6"
Green	2 C & 2 Cr	8" x 10"
	2 F & 2 Fr	6" x 7"
Rust	2 D	6" x 8"
	2 G	4" x 6"
Multicolor print	1 H	4" x 4"

The following steps are for raw-edge fusible appliqué. Use a photocopier to enlarge the pattern 200% for a 16" x 20" block, or to any size you desire.

1. Use freezer paper or tracing paper to make a master pattern of the block on page 31.

2. Fold the background square into quarters and press. Use the pressed lines as guides for centering your appliqué pieces.

3. Trace each individual pattern piece onto the paper side of your favorite fusible web. (For pieces that will be covered by another piece, add a ¼" allowance to only the portion that will be covered.) Rough-cut each of the fusible web pieces.

4. Following the manufacturer's directions, iron the fusible web pattern pieces to the wrong sides of the appropriate fabrics.

5. Cut out all the fabric pieces on the drawn lines and carefully peel off the paper backing.

6. Position each appliqué piece on the background square. Fuse the pieces to the background according to the manufacturer's instructions.

7. Place a piece of freezer paper behind your background square to stabilize it for sewing.

8. Machine sew (in alphabetical order) the raw edges of each piece with a narrow zigzag stitch in matching thread. Tear away the stabilizer when your appliqué is complete.

9. Press the appliquéd block, then trim it to 16½" x 20½", which includes seam allowances.

Template Tip

I usually mark one side of my plastic templates with the patch letters, then turn the templates over and mark the other side with the reverse template letters. This way, I only have to make one template for both pieces.

Shining Light

To make a 16" x 20" block,
enlarge this pattern 200%.
(Permission to copy as needed
for non-commercial use.)

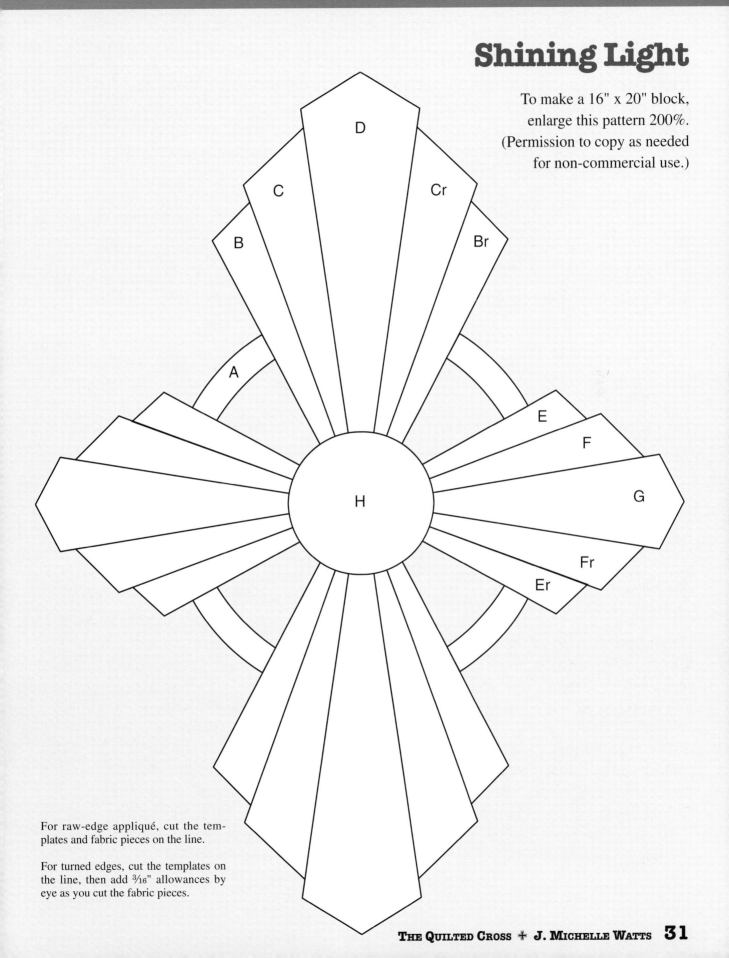

For raw-edge appliqué, cut the templates and fabric pieces on the line.

For turned edges, cut the templates on the line, then add 3/16" allowances by eye as you cut the fabric pieces.

Cross Your Heart

Finished block 10"

1 appliqué piece

(pattern on page 34)

CROSS YOUR HEART (30" x 50"), by the author. Everyone's heard the phrase "Cross your heart." It's used to seal a promise.

Use this simple block to make a quilt for someone you love. Try making a baby quilt, using lots of bright, cheerful, happy prints, or a special Valentine quilt in red and white.

Cutting Instructions (one block)

Fabric	Cut	Cut from scrap
White print	1 square	12" x 12"
Black print	1 A	9½" x 9½"

The following steps are for raw-edge fusible appliqué. Use a photocopier to enlarge the pattern 121% for a 10" block (or any size you desire).

1. Use freezer paper or tracing paper to make a master pattern of the block on page 34.

2. Fold the background square into quarters and press. Use the pressed lines as guides for centering your appliqué pieces.

3. Trace each individual pattern piece onto the paper side of your favorite fusible web. (For pieces that will be covered by another piece, add a ¼" allowance only to the portion that will be covered.) Rough-cut each of the fusible web pieces.

4. Following the manufacturer's directions, iron the fusible web pattern pieces to the wrong sides of the appropriate fabrics.

5. Cut out all the fabric pieces on the drawn lines and carefully peel off the paper backing.

6. Position each appliqué piece on the background square. Fuse the pieces to the background according to the manufacturer's instructions.

7. Place a piece of freezer paper behind your background square to stabilize it for sewing.

8. Machine sew (in alphabetical order) the raw edges of each piece with a narrow zigzag stitch in matching thread. Tear away the stabilizer when your appliqué is complete.

9. Press the appliquéd block, then trim it to 10½" square, which includes seam allowances.

SCRAPPY HEARTS (50" x 62"), by the author. Each scrappy heart block is sashed with different strips

Cross Your Heart

To make a 10" block, enlarge this pattern 121%
(Permission to copy as needed for non-commercial use.)

For raw-edge appliqué, cut the templates and fabric pieces on the line.

For turned edges, cut the templates on the line, then add ³⁄₁₆" allowances by eye as you cut the fabric pieces.

Santa Cruz Sampler

20 finished blocks 15"

SANTA CRUZ SAMPLER (78" x 96"), by the author. Twenty different appliquéd cross blocks create this sampler with a Southwestern flair.

Santa Cruz Sampler

The blocks are numbered from 1 to 20, starting at the top-left block. To make all 20 blocks, you will need 5¼ yards of background fabric. Each background square will be cut 17" x 17". I selected ½ yard of each of 10 different fabrics for my appliqué pieces. If you decide to make all 20 blocks with the sashing, you will need 2¼ yards of navy and 2¾ yards for the backgroound.

Appliqué Instructions

The following steps are for raw-edge fusible appliqué. Use a photocopier to enlarge the pattern 200% for a 15 ½" block (or any size you desire).

1. Use freezer paper or tracing paper to make a master pattern of the block (page 11).

2. Fold the background square into quarters and press. Use the pressed lines as guides for centering your appliqué pieces.

3. Trace each individual pattern piece onto the paper side of your favorite fusible web. (For pieces that will be covered by another piece, add a ¼" allowance only to the portion that will be covered.) Rough-cut each of the fusible web pieces.

4. Following the manufacturer's directions, iron the fusible web pattern pieces to the wrong sides of the appropriate fabrics.

5. Cut out all the fabric pieces on the drawn lines and carefully peel off the paper backing.

6. Position each appliqué piece on the background square. Fuse the pieces to the background according to the manufacturer's instructions.

7. Place a piece of freezer paper behind your background square to stabilize it for sewing.

8. Machine sew (in alphabetical order) the raw edges of each piece with a narrow zigzag stitch in matching thread. Tear away the stabilizer when your appliqué is complete.

9. Press the appliquéd block, then trim it to 15½", which includes seam allowances.

Santa Cruz Sashing

Full-sized
for 15" blocks
(Permission to copy as needed
for non-commercial use.)

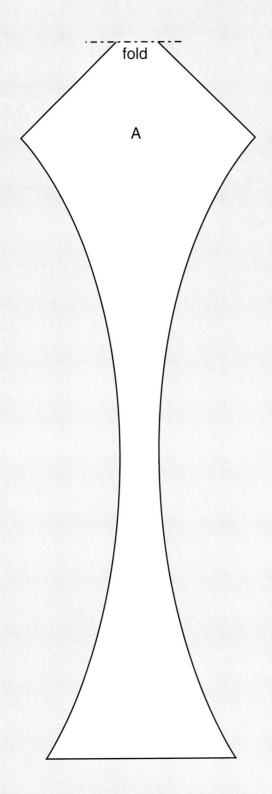

fold

A

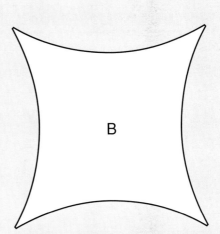

B

Sashing Instructions

Cut navy cornerstones 3½" x 3½".
Cut background sashing strips 3½" x 15½".

Cutting Instructions (one block)		
Fabric	**Cut**	**From one scrap**
Background	B	3" x 3"
Navy	A	3" x 16"

You can cut (13) B from a 3" x 40" strip.
You can cut (13) A from a 16" x 40" strip.

Block 1

1 appliqué piece

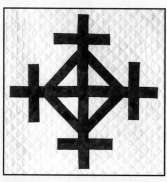

To make a 15" block, enlarge this pattern 200%. (Permission to copy as needed for non-commercial use.)

I have seen several variations of this type of cross design in old tinwork. I also found a similar design on a heraldic cross Web site.

Cutting Instructions (one block)

Fabric	Cut	From one scrap
Background	Square	17" x 17"
Wine	1 A	15" x 15"

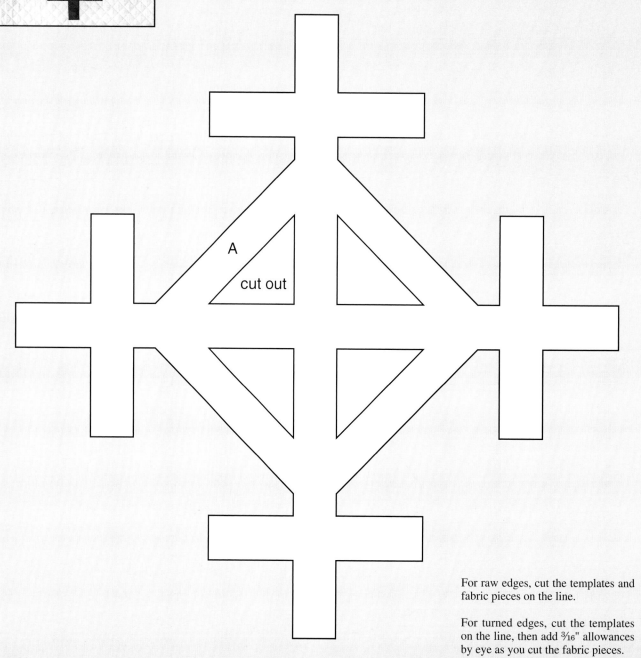

A

cut out

For raw edges, cut the templates and fabric pieces on the line.

For turned edges, cut the templates on the line, then add ³⁄₁₆" allowances by eye as you cut the fabric pieces.

This cross design was inspired by a stone carving on the wall of a building in Texas.

Block 2

3 appliqué pieces

Cutting Instructions (one block)

Fabric	Cut	From one scrap
Background	Square	17" x 17"
Lt. turquoise	1 A	14" x 14"
Terra cotta	1 B	12" x 12"
Grape	1 C	9" x 9"

To make a 15" block, enlarge this pattern 200%. (Permission to copy as needed for non-commercial use.)

For raw edges, cut the templates and fabric pieces on the line.

For turned edges, cut the templates on the line, then add ³⁄₁₆" allowances by eye as you cut the fabric pieces.

Block 3

10 appliqué pieces

This design was inspired by a Celtic cross.

To make a 15" block, enlarge this pattern 200%. (Permission to copy as needed for non-commercial use.)

Cutting Instructions (one block)

Fabric	Cut	From one scrap
Background	Square	17" x 17"
Gold	4 A	6" x 7"
Grape	1 B	15" x 15"
Wine	4 C	4" x 10"
	1 D	2" x 2"

I saw this cross design on a crown pictured in a book about Madonnas of Mexico.

Block 4
22 appliqué pieces

Cutting Instructions (one block)

Fabric	Cut	From one scrap
Background	Square	17" x 17"
Gold	1 A	14½" x 14½"
Red	16 B	4" x 15"
Md. turquoise	4 C	3" x 3"
	1 D	2" x 2"

To make a 15" block, enlarge this pattern 200%. (Permission to copy as needed for non-commercial use.)

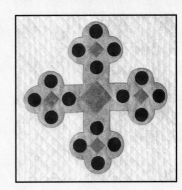

Block 5

2 appliqué pieces

To make a 15" block, enlarge this pattern 200%. (Permission to copy as needed for non-commercial use.)

This cross was inspired by an old wrought-iron light fixture. I took part of the shape of the curved iron and repeated it to form the cross design.

Cutting Instructions (one block)

Fabric	Cut	From one scrap
Background	Square	17" x 17"
Terra cotta	1 A	15" x 15"
Dk. turquoise	1 B	3" x 3"

The iron hinge on an old trunk was the inspiration for the outer cross shape. Notice that the right half of the block is the mirror image of the left half.

Block 6
3 appliqué pieces

Cutting Instructions (one block)

Fabric	Cut	From one scrap
Background	Square	17" x 17"
Navy	1 A	14½" x 14½"
Md. turquoise	1 B	12" x 12"
Gold	1 C	3" x 5"

To make a 15" block, enlarge this pattern 200%. (Permission to copy as needed for non-commercial use.)

Block 7

2 appliqué pieces

A Mexican tile was the inspiration for this cross.

To make a 15" block, enlarge this pattern 200%. (Permission to copy as needed for non-commercial use.)

Cutting Instructions (one block)

Fabric	Cut	From one scrap
Background	Square	17" x 17"
Dk. turquoise	1 A	16" x 16"
Red	1 B	11" x 11"

A beadwork design on a Native American costume at the Gathering of the Nations in Albuquerque, New Mexico, sparked the idea for this geometric cross.

Block 8

9 appliqué pieces

Cutting Instructions (one block)

Fabric	Cut	From one scrap
Background	Square	17" x 17"
Grape	4 B	7" x 37"
Lt. turquoise	4 A	5½" x 28"
	1 C	2¼" x 2¼"

To make a 15" block, enlarge this pattern 200%. (Permission to copy as needed for non-commercial use.)

A   B   C

Block 9

10 appliqué pieces

This cross was based on a Mexican stamp used to decorate pottery, cloth, paper, or skin.

To make a 15" block, enlarge this pattern 200%. (Permission to copy as needed for non-commercial use.)

Cutting Instructions (one block)

Fabric	Cut	From one scrap
Background	Square	17" x 17"
Green	1 A	15" x 15"
Gold	5 B	5" x 25"
Red	4 C	4" x 4"

This ornate cross design was inspired by an iron fence.

Block 10
11 appliqué pieces

Cutting Instructions (one block)

Fabric	Cut	From one scrap
Background	Square	17" x 17"
Grape	4 A	4" x 8"
	1 C	7" x 7"
Wine	4 B	8" x 30"
Gold	1 D	4" x 4"
Terra cotta	1 E	3¼" x 3¼"

To make a 15" block, enlarge this pattern 200%. (Permission to copy as needed for non-commercial use.)

Block 11

7 appliqué pieces

The center diamond of this cross was based on a hand-painted Mexican tile. I added the wedge-shaped cross arms to create a unique cross.

To make a 15" block, enlarge this pattern 200%. (Permission to copy as needed for non-commercial use.)

Cutting Instructions (one block)

Fabric	Cut	From one scrap
Background	Square	17" x 17"
Navy	4 A	5" x 18"
Green	1 B	9" x 9"
Wine	1 C	5" x 5"
Gold	1 D	4" x 4"

I think this simple shape resembles a floral design, which was inspired by one I saw in a book about Madonnas of Mexico.

Block 12
9 appliqué pieces

Cutting Instructions (one block)

Fabric	Cut	From one scrap
Background	Square	17" x 17"
Lt. turquoise	4 A	4" x 7"
	1 C	4" x 4"
Wine	4 B	7" x 26"

To make a 15" block, enlarge this pattern 200%. (Permission to copy as needed for non-commercial use.)

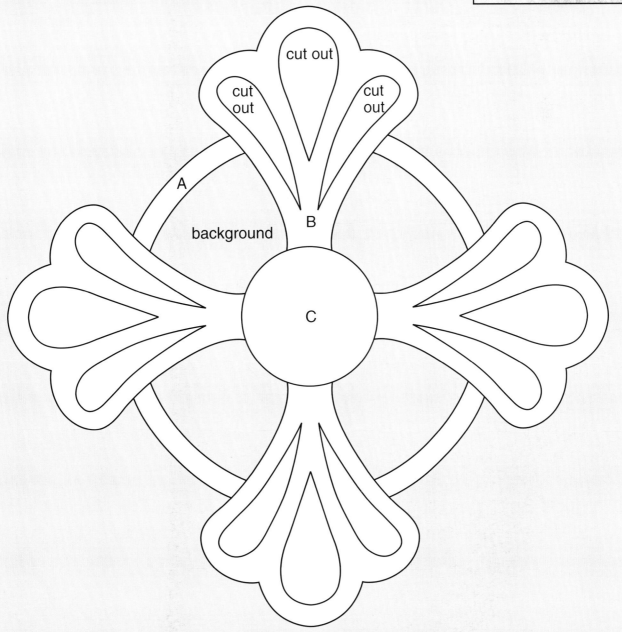

cut out

cut out

cut out

A

background

B

C

Block 13

2 appliqué pieces

A simple cross shape from an old wooden door was the inspiration for this pattern.

To make a 15" block, enlarge this pattern 200%. (Permission to copy as needed for non-commercial use.)

Cutting Instructions (one block)		
Fabric	**Cut**	**From one scrap**
Background	Square	17" x 17"
Md. turquoise	1 A	15" x 15"
Red	1 B	14" x 14"

Block 14

7 appliqué pieces

The outline of this cross was inspired by a silver belt. Additional shapes inside and outside the main cross enhance the design.

Cutting Instructions (one block)

Fabric	Cut	From one scrap
Background	Square	17" x 17"
Dk. turquoise	4 A	5" x 11"
	1 D	11" x 11"
Gold	1 B	15" x 15"
Lt. turquoise	1 C	14" x 14"

To make a 16" x 20" block, enlarge this pattern 200%. (Permission to copy as needed for non-commercial use.)

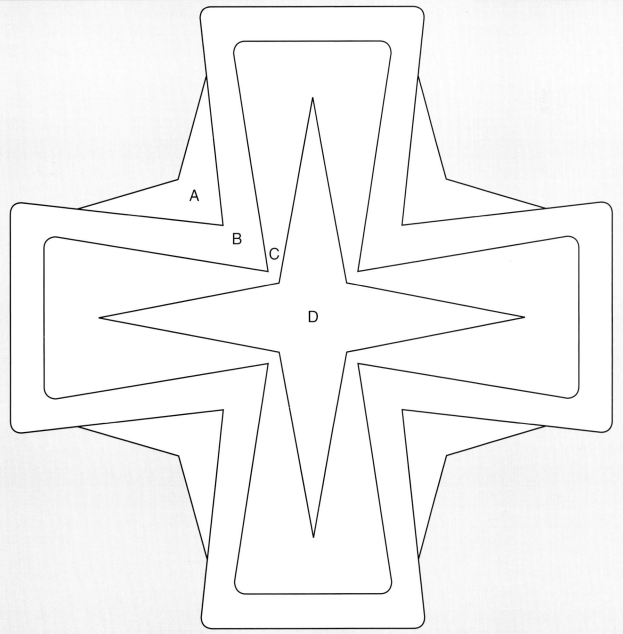

Block 15

2 appliqué pieces

The outer shape of this cross was painted on the wall in an old mission. The center design is from another wrought-iron shape I saw in New Mexico.

To make a 15" block, enlarge this pattern 200%. (Permission to copy as needed for non-commercial use.)

Cutting Instructions (one block)

Fabric	Cut	From one scrap
Background	Square	17" x 17"
Terra cotta	1 A	14" x 14"
Lt. turquoise	1 B	8" x 8"

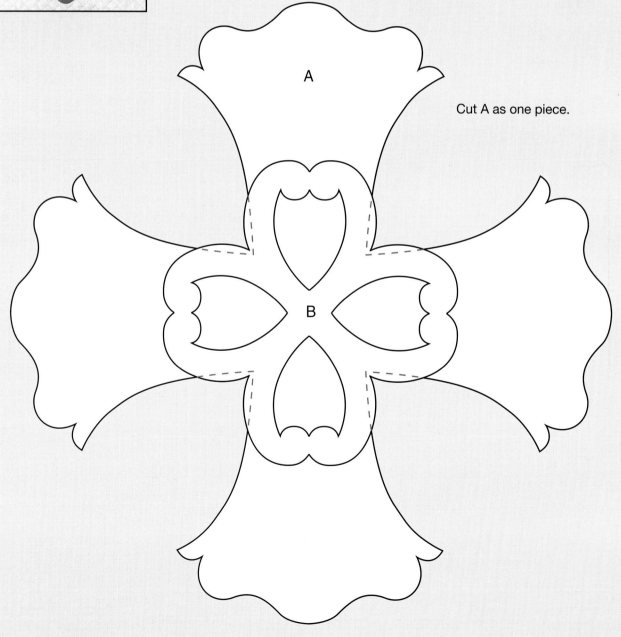

Cut A as one piece.

This design came from a Mexican stamp design used to decorate pottery, skin, cloth, or paper.

Block 16

5 appliqué pieces

Cutting Instructions (one block)

Fabric	Cut	From one scrap
Background	Square	17" x 17"
Md. turquoise	4 A	15" x 15"
Navy	1 B	4" x 4"

To make a 15" block, enlarge this pattern 200%. (Permission to copy as needed for non-commercial use.)

Block 17

15 appliqué pieces

To make a 15" block, enlarge this pattern 200%. (Permission to copy as needed for non-commercial use.)

This design was inspired by a tinwork cross with stained glass accents. The tinwork was heavily stamped, and colored glass shapes sparkled against the silver.

Cutting Instructions (one block)

Fabric	Cut	From one scrap
Background	Square	17" x 17"
Navy	1 A	15" x 15"
Lt. turquoise	1 B	10" x 10"
Wine	8 C	4" x 20"
Gold	5 D	2" x 11"

Cut A as one piece.

I have seen similar cross shapes in painted or stamped terra cotta tiles.

Block 18

6 appliqué pieces

Cutting Instructions (one block)

Fabric	Cut	From one scrap
Background	Square	17" x 17"
Grape	1 A	15" x 15"
Md. turquoise	4 B	6" x 6"
Terra cotta	1C	11" x 11"

To make a 15" block, enlarge this pattern 200%. (Permission to copy as needed for non-commercial use.)

Block 19

11 appliqué pieces

I came across a calendar about Catherine the Great. It was filled with beautiful pictures but, of course, the only thing that caught my attention was a cross pendant worn by Catherine. This is a simple variation of her pendant.

To make a 15" block, enlarge this pattern 200%. (Permission to copy as needed for non-commercial use.)

Cutting Instructions (one block)

Fabric	Cut	From one scrap
Background	Square	17" x 17"
Gold	1 A	9" x 9"
Green	5 B	5" x 25"
Red	5 C	4" x 20"

Cut A as one piece.

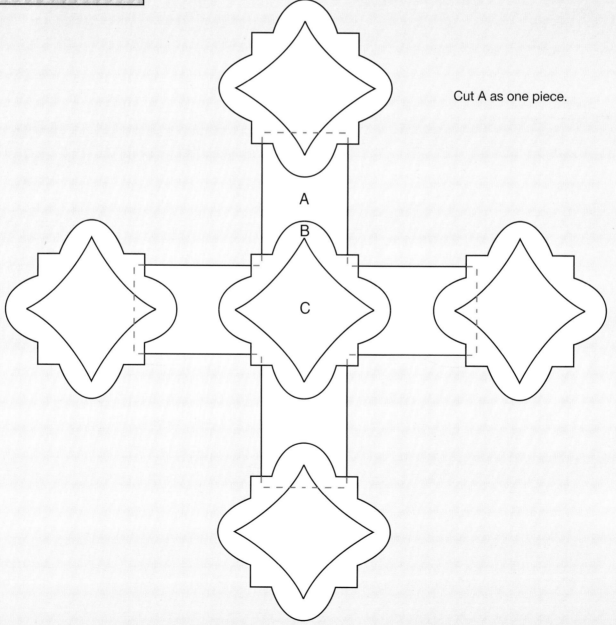

Block 20

6 appliqué pieces

I really like the soft, rounded shape of this cross, which was inspired by a design carved in stone on the front of the San Antonio Missions National Historical Park in San Antonio, Texas.

Cutting Instructions (one block)

Fabric	Cut	From one scrap
Background	Square	17" x 17"
Wine	1 A	15" x 15"
Gold	4 B	5" x 16"
Gold	1 C	4" x 4"

To make a 15" block, enlarge this pattern 200%. (Permission to copy as needed for non-commercial use.)

Embroidered Crosses
Spanish Cross Sampler

Finished block 9" x 11"

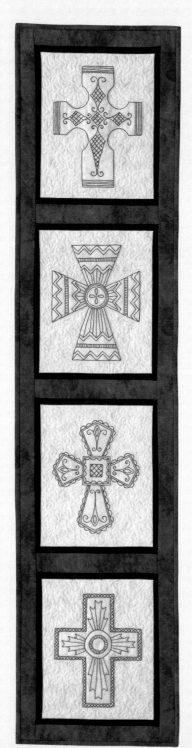

These cross patterns, inspired by a variety of different Spanish colonial arts and crafts, are easy to hand embroider by using a simple straight stitch or backstitch. If you are up for a challenge, try using a black background and a light gold or cream thread for the embroidery. It's a challenge because it is difficult to see your drawn design on the black fabric, but the end result will be spectacular.

SPANISH CROSS SAMPLER BROWN (27" x 31"), by Marion Wessel, Roswell, New Mexico. Marion embroidered each block in a different color.

Making the blocks

Follow these steps for each of the four designs:

1. Trace the pattern on a piece of tracing paper for easier handling.

2. Cut a 11" x 13" background rectangle. Center the design on the rectangle and trace lightly.

3. Embroider the design with a backstitch and two strands of embroidery thread.

4. After the embroidery is complete, trim the block to 9½" x 11½".

Spanish Cross Sampler (13" x 56"), by the author. I learned to hand embroider from my grandmother when I was a small child, so when I started creating crosses, it seemed only logical to design several to embroider.

Embroidered
Block 1
Full-sized
pattern

Embroidered Block 2

Full-sized
pattern

Embroidered
Block 3
Full-sized
pattern

Embroidered
Block 4
Full-sized
pattern

About the Author

Michelle's talent for designing quilts and wearable art has led her to many successful endeavors. She designs and markets a line of Southwestern quilt patterns. She has exhibited her wearable art creations in several American Quilter's Society fashion shows, the 1999 Fairfield Fashion Show, and ARTWEAR 2002. Her quilts and wearable art have also been shown in galleries, museums, and quilt shows throughout the United States. She teaches, lectures, and provides special exhibits for quilt groups across the country.

Michelle lives in Roswell, New Mexico, with her husband, Randy, daughter, Jessica, and two dogs. When she's not quilting, Michelle enjoys spending time with her friends and family and playing with her pet prairie dogs, Bubba and Max.

To get in touch with the author, you can call her at 505-622-1826, or e-mail her at ffos@rt66.com.

Other AQS Books

This is only a small selection of the books available from the American Quilter's Society. AQS books are known worldwide for timely topics, clear writing, beautiful color photos, and accurate illustrations and patterns. The following books are available from your local bookseller, quilt shop, or public library.

#6408   US$22.95

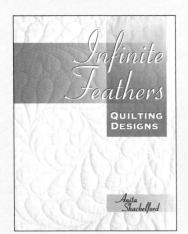

#6072   US$25.95

#6298   US$24.95

#6300   US$24.95

#6001   US$21.95

#6077   US$24.95

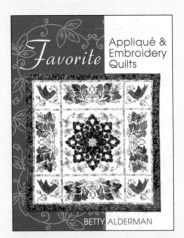

#6410   US$19.95

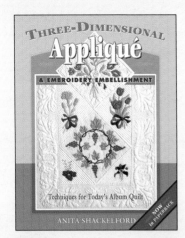

#6292   US$24.95

#6213   US$24.95

LOOK *for these books nationally.* CALL **1-800-626-5420**
or VISIT *our Web site at* **www.AQSquilt.com**